# ANIMAL LIFE STORIES

# THE DEER

Kingfisher Books, Grisewood & Dempsey Ltd,
Elsley House, 24–30 Great Titchfield Street,
London W1P 7AD.

First published in this edition in 1988
by Kingfisher Books.
The colour illustrations in this book are
taken from *Wildlife Library: The Deer*
originally published in hardback in 1979.
Reprinted 1988, 1990
Copyright © Grisewood & Dempsey Ltd, 1988

BRITISH LIBRARY CATALOGUING IN PUBLICATION DATA
Royston, Angela
 The deer. – (Picture Kingfisher). –
 (Animal life stories).
 1. Red deer – Juvenile literature
 I. Title  II. Series
 599.73'57   QL737.U55
ISBN 0 86272 354 X

Edited by Jacqui Bailey
Designed by Ben White
Cover design by David Jefferis
Cover illustration by Steve Holden/*John Martin &
Artists Ltd*
Phototypeset by Southern Positives & Negatives (SPAN),
Lingfield, Surrey
Printed in Spain

ANIMAL LIFE STORIES

# THE DEER

By Angela Royston

Illustrated by Bernard Robinson

Kingfisher Books

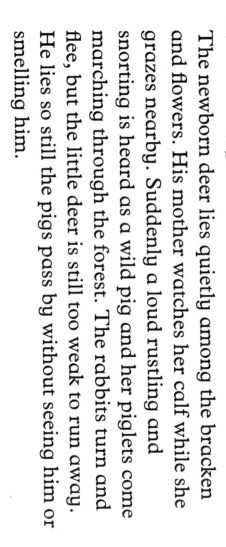

The newborn deer lies quietly among the bracken and flowers. His mother watches her calf while she grazes nearby. Suddenly a loud rustling and snorting is heard as a wild pig and her piglets come marching through the forest. The rabbits turn and flee, but the little deer is still too weak to run away. He lies so still the pigs pass by without seeing him or smelling him.

Night is falling before the mother comes back to feed her calf. He stands shakily to suck her milk, then he lies close to her warm fur in the dark.

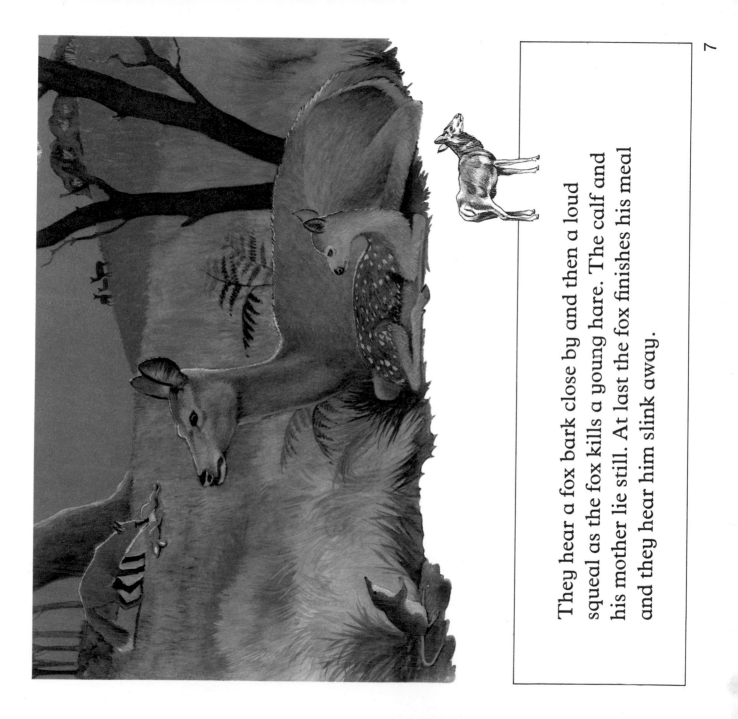

They hear a fox bark close by and then a loud squeal as the fox kills a young hare. The calf and his mother lie still. At last the fox finishes his meal and they hear him slink away.

The calves in the herd grow quickly, playing together while the females graze close by. Female deer are called hinds and male deer, stags. All the stags live in another part of the forest. One day a buzzard appears in the sky. The old hind who leads the herd barks in alarm and the others swiftly follow her to the safety of the trees.

A year passes and the calf becomes a young stag. He no longer needs his mother's milk and eats leaves and grass instead. One misty autumn morning he hears the male stags bellowing through the trees. Suddenly a big adult male appears, with huge branching antlers.

The big male snorts and swings around to face the young stag. Frightened, the young stag runs into the forest. He swims a river and runs far from the herd. He wanders for several days, then meets a herd of young stags who let him join them.

The stag is now six years old and again it is spring. His thick winter coat feels too hot and he rolls in a muddy pool to cool down. Then he rubs himself against a tree, pulling out tufts of loose hair.

That evening as he goes to the river to drink a chattering squirrel startles him. One of his antlers hits a tree and with a loud crack it breaks off.

Soon the other antler falls off and he is left with two little stumps. But the stumps swell up and by the end of summer, new, bigger antlers have grown.

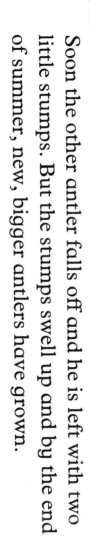

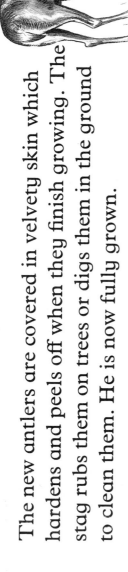

The new antlers are covered in velvety skin which hardens and peels off when they finish growing. The stag rubs them on trees or digs them in the ground to clean them. He is now fully grown.

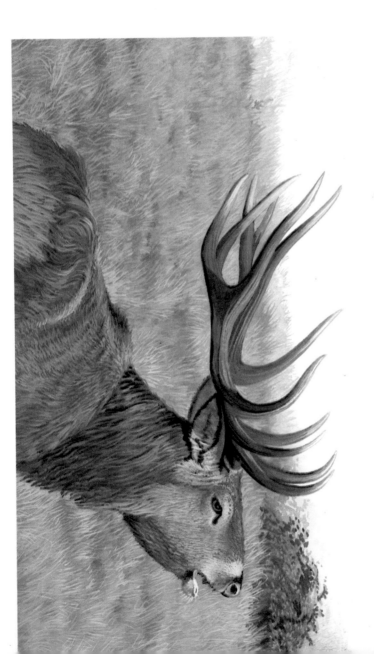

It is autumn and the stag is restless. He leaves the other young stags to look for a herd of hinds. He hears the sound of a stag coughing and with a loud bellow he bursts out of the trees and into a clearing, where an old stag is grazing with a herd of females. He paws the ground and digs his antlers into the grass to show the old stag how strong he is.

The old stag snorts in reply, then both stags lower their heads and charge. Their antlers lock together and they struggle against each other. They stagger and pull apart, panting. Then they grunt, paw the ground and rush at each other again.

As the old stag slips and falls forward, the young challenger lunges and stabs him with his antlers. Defeated, the old stag runs away, leaving the herd with the stronger young stag.

The stag guards his herd of females, roaring to frighten away any other stag who comes near. For ten days he mates with the hinds in the herd, then he leaves them. The stag is tired now and thin, and he needs to rest before winter comes. In spring the hinds will give birth to new calves and next winter the stag will find another herd of hinds.

## More About Deer

There are more than fifty different kinds of deer. The largest is the Alaskan bull moose which is bigger than a horse, and the smallest is the South American pudu which is as small as a corgi dog. The deer in this story are red deer. Male red deer are bigger than the females and the females do not grow any antlers.

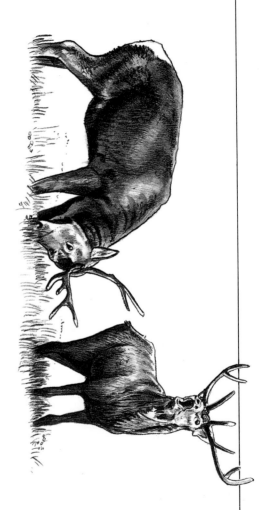

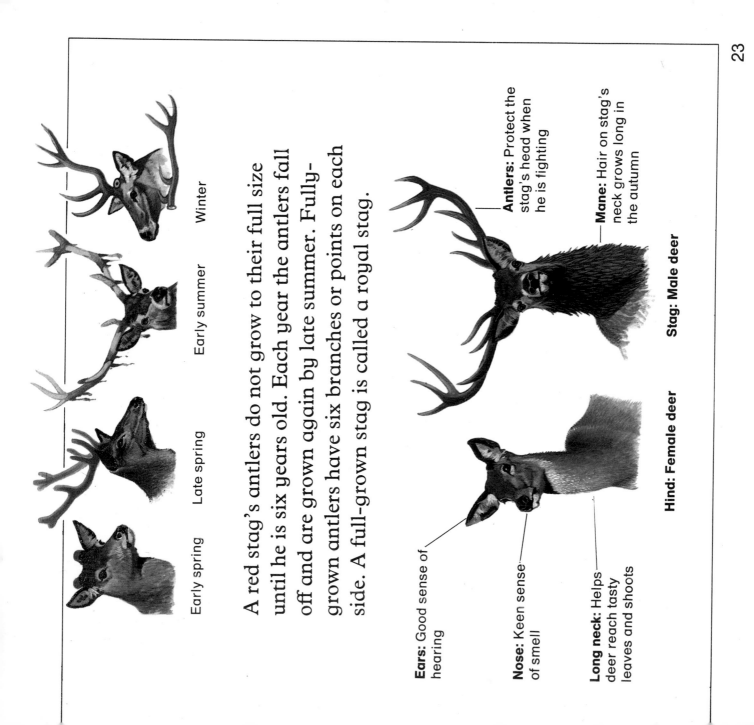

Early spring   Late spring   Early summer   Winter

A red stag's antlers do not grow to their full size until he is six years old. Each year the antlers fall off and are grown again by late summer. Fully-grown antlers have six branches or points on each side. A full-grown stag is called a royal stag.

**Antlers:** Protect the stag's head when he is fighting

**Mane:** Hair on stag's neck grows long in the autumn

**Stag: Male deer**

**Ears:** Good sense of hearing

**Nose:** Keen sense of smell

**Long neck:** Helps deer reach tasty leaves and shoots

**Hind: Female deer**

# Some Special Words

**Antlers** A branch-like growth of bone on the head of a male deer. As they grow they are covered in a velvety skin which peels and falls off, leaving full-grown shiny antlers. A red deer's antlers are more than a metre long.

**Buzzard** A bird which swoops to the ground to kill young or small animals for food.

**Calf** A baby or young deer.

**Fawn** Another name for a baby or young deer.

**Herd** A group of deer who live together. Deer live in separate herds, either all hinds and calves or all stags.

**Hind** A female deer.

**Reindeer** These are a kind of tame deer used by people in the far northern lands.

**Stag** A male deer.